# All Present, Unaccounted For

# ALL PRESENT, UNACCOUNTED FOR

Images from a war, and after ...

✠

By **Robert Flanagan**

**Connemara Press**
**Winchester, Virginia**
**connemarapress.org**

International Standard Book Number 0-87012-896-5
Library of Congress Control Number 2018911902
Printed in the United States of America
Copyright © 2018 by Robert Flanagan
Winchester, VA
All Rights Reserved
2018




McClain Printing Company
Parsons, WV 26287
www.mcclainprinting.com
2018

# Contents

## Page Number

# Contents, continued ...

# Poems' Publication Data

A number of the enclosed poems, as individual works, have been published in various magazines, journals, newspapers and other word-streams.

"Vicarious Hero," "Sleight of Hand" and "Pastorale" in *phoebe* (George Mason Univ. literary journal), April 1979

"Mayday" in *The Journal Messenger* newspaper, Manassas, Va., Sep. 14, 1979

"Street of Hondas" in *phoebe,* Winter 1980

"Wire" and "Semi-Private Mirages" in *Crop Dust* literary magazine, Spring 1980

"Semi-Private Mirages" in *phoebe*, April 1980

"Survivals" and "Wire" in *Adventures in Hell*, book, 1990

"Street of Hondas, " "Sleight of Hand" and "Another Kind of Understanding" in *Vietnam Generation* **Vol. 6, Nrs. 1&2, 1994**

# About the Author and This Work

Robert Flanagan was born in Mississippi in 1936. Two younger siblings died early; his father was killed in 1943. The Depression and World War II inevitably framed his youthful maturation years.

Entering the Marines in 1953, he served seven years in the U.S., Panama and on the Caribbean and Mediterranean seas. Leaving the Corps in 1960, he joined the Army Security Agency (intelligence), serving 16 more years, 13 of them abroad in Eritrea (Ethiopia), Germany, Viet Nam, Italy and Morocco.

He retired from the Army in 1976, a Chief Warrant Officer. Then followed 13 years at firms building electronics collection systems (government contract work) and, attending evening classes, completed a bachelor's and two graduate degrees; then retired again to teach English, American Literature and Creative Writing at three colleges in Virginia.

Their children grown and away, he and wife Julia moved in 1986 to West Virginia, where he retired a third time to write. For 19 years he wrote a weekly newspaper column for local papers, and wrote hundreds of articles, stories, reviews and poems for publication. In the period 2001-2012 he published six books: two of selected pieces from his newspaper column, "Bits & Pieces"; a book of short fiction, *Peripheral Visions;* and "The ASA Trilogy," a tale of the Army Security Agency in Viet Nam and the Cold War. The trilogy (a fictionalized, lengthy memoir) is the ultimate fulfillment of 47 years of journal-keeping, outline, layout, writing, editing, re-writing, re-editing, *ad infinitum*.

✠

The war poetry began with the journal-keeping in 1964 Viet Nam, the same recorded memoirs that produced the trilogy. Many of the poems emerged in the 1970s-1980s as work produced for the MFA (Master's in Fine Art: Creative Writing) at George Mason University, Fairfax, Virginia, but took another 35 years to ferment into what the author felt was a body of work worthy of publication.

A second collection of poetry is being assembled for publication, but not of war-related subject matter. This second collection evokes images and memories from the extensive travels in many foreign cultures which the author has enjoyed, primarily due to his military career. Military assignments got him there; his writer's/poet's eye found expression in all about him. There are, additionally, several poems of an experimental format, some "concrete" poems, "found" poems and similar transformations.

All the writer's books are available on his website, connemarapress.org, on Amazon.com and through most bookstores.

# Dedication

Extending the protocol of dedicating my writings to those closest to me — first book, *Bits & Pieces,* to wife Julia; the second, *Peripheral Visions,* to our four children; third-through-fifth (The ASA Trilogy) to the Viet Nam vets about whom the books were written, and the sixth, *Lesser Bits, Greater Pieces*,   to the 10 grandchildren — I offer this collection of poems, images and memories, book 7, in homage to the children of my grandchildren:

> Ethan
> Aidan
> Ryann
> Lana
> Grayson
> Felix
> Dexter
> Gabriel

And my grateful thanks to the generosity with time and skill of my artist son, Liam, for the map art on the cover and ConnemaraPress logo (family crest) on the title page.

## VACATION IN VIETNAM, 1964

Obscene poster, a projection.
Sly humor, subsumed in reality.
Foolish farmers
and fishermen, entitled to be foolish
if they choose,
witness this slight with fear and suspicion,
but no understanding.

Small brown sappers, hard core
of the VC Three-Ninety-Fifth Battalion —
and equally vulgar aspirants to the title —
dash ashore in the night wash of the South
China Sea at Vung Tau
orchestrated, choreographed ... not a ballet:
a quiet time-lapse jitterbug.

They don't know that alien planners
will name this place in-country R-and-R.
That the sand will become in time
a gritty bed for oil-daubed pink bodies —
fresh from the fetid jungle growth
of II and III Corps — where sun
can blanch out the heat rash, immersion foot
and crotch rot,
the fungus of un-washed bodies.

The wave-stroked sand will become cursory
beds for frenzied couplings
with much-sought-after nurses, Donut
Dollies and various whores.   No,
they don't know.   They think
this sand is their's because of birthright
and they pay for it again
in blood — their's and our's.   But their
tiny Michelin footprints
will wash out on the tide with their dreams.

I know.   My colonel
told me their cause is not just.

## After XXIII by Rexroth (Hitomaro)

All the Asian paths
have blended to a sameness.
It may be autumn on this mountain for all I know;
the leaves are gone
and orange is the only agent color.
Trails are no longer hidden;
only the living, well disguised.

Any girl I can find is one dollar in scrip
and already her bones
will have begun to disintegrate.


**XXIII**
The colored leaves
have hidden the paths
on the autumn mountain.
How can I find my girl
wandering on ways I do not know?
— Kakinomoto no Hitomaro —

from: *100 Poems From the Japanese*
— Kenneth Rexroth —

## A Barely Credible Relationship

On his knees, deep in foliage chaff
red with iron soil and iron blood,
dog tags taped for silence
against his ebony chest,
grotesque how he cries for Whitey
who gave him only bad history.

He flings an arm toward the static treeline,
a place too hot to sustain life, not
an impotent threat,
the flash suppressor ineffective,
untempered with sorrow.

Only mercenaries, serving practiced masters
through protocols of innocence,
will not prolong the fleeing life
and still will cry
under such incredible liens.

I wished I could live
one day inside
his grandfather's 90-year-old memory,
sail down the bitter slaving sea lanes
on the tides of his days.

From Minneapolis to Memphis,
floating Huck Finn routes instead
off Hannibal's lofty bluffs;
feel the bondage chain,
know the whip,
sense the coming noose of outraged guilt.

Though he never wore the medal
he might have earned with different skin,
didn't drink the victory brew,
share the praise of printed word,
they cannot remove that
appellation of acknowledgment:

*Combat veteran!*

And now whole conflicts later
this product of untempered passions
casts aside all life's lessons —
not having read history,
destined to repeat it —
and gives of himself
in common cause:

*Soldier.*

## A Gifted Mediocrity

I wear still your accusation
with its myriad nuances
like another bit of colored ribbon
marking my descent
into a subtler depravity.

*Go on! Go to war!*
I could as well have been
ordered to the supermarket
in the ire of your frustration.

The tendrils of conscience have dried,
their elasticity gone brittle,
and beliefs and dreams died,
with the long column of youth
a fragment of the past,
like acrylic vultures' wings,
keeps me to the task
and will not sanction my failure.

Wanton incivilities,
practiced on an egalitarian scale,
reduce this pathos to fiction —
a kind of reality.

## Not A Cowboy In Sight

I tell you about *Ranch Hand* and you want to talk
cows and the price of steak.
Household budgets are more your concern
and coupons
never appear on page one.

Cattle fare badly in the jungle,
I insist.   Branding and roping are fantasies
of the trail.   The chores of these Hands,
instead, was obliteration
of that trail, that jungle, all greening things.
And you should know . . . they did this
believing.

*Brazil!*  you shout, elated at your own perception,
again
*Argentina!*  You know about vaqueros,
the Pampas.

Written across a slate of green beyond our vision
in a fine, deadly mist the words *Agent Orange*.
The images this innocuous phrase suggests
are diverse, second-level symbolic: tall
career-oriented faceless men
dressed in local colors,
shadows in alleyways,
embassy backrooms.

Cargo chutes blossoming
over southern drop zones.
Floridanita,
her famous anti-fag smile framed
behind a pitcher of juice, while against a cinerama
screen of sweat and synthetic coupling,
short fat men tout their pimpled charges, leering.

A prime bit of sophistry fit for the occasion
occurs to me, but you bruise easily.
You don't find Anita funny
and you don't know what a drop zone is.

Your vision still
admits no white, stateless beds in rows,
no myopic, twitching glances
never held quite still; no debilitating
stumbling walk-around, raging
distorted children.

It is pointless even for me to mention to you
the most chilling confession a veteran ever uttered:
*I don't know if I died in Vietnam or not . . . yet.*

The flavor of prime rib, fresh on your mind's
tongue, and the romance of pulp
magazines and John Wayne flicks
circumvent your practiced compassion.

# In Name Only

Breakfast yields to black humor.   Unknowing
children devour crunchy sweetnesses
of jingle-flavored grains.

Deciphering cardboard boxes,
hearing the innocent appelation on filial lips,
watching rhythmical jaws
mulching insipid puffed cerialia,
a sickness of soul
belittles the momentary sickness of body.

The Captive Greek
squatting in the burnt-over field
gave birth to the blasphemy:
gestation was in snipered, booby-trapped
impotence
(conception, a long line of empire).
Peer pressure jokes die hard of shame.

Harnessed to the 11th Cav track
the barbecued remains (euphemism, plural)
were wrenched from the shallow spider hole
hidden under creeper vines.
Napalm had cooked their midsections to ripeness,
their torsos to crumbling dissolution:
in the angle of the trap both broke at the beltline.
Matching tops and bottoms was unlikely:

*All the king's horses, and*
*All the king's men . . .*

the charred limbs,
Calder-wired caricatures with outstretched
clutching
claws, invoke some disinterested God
or some equally ineffectual party leader.

The Captive Greek spoiled for me forever
there in that pasture of hell
the grace and pleasure of early morning meals:

*Crispy critters,*
an irrevocable obscenity
not displaced by time or distance.

## Not My Kind Of War

Early days, more French yet than ours,
the war loomed just outside city limits.
Off the plane, like tourists in Toledo,
rumors got heavy play:

> *There's a bounty on ASA.   Don't go over the
> Bien Hoa bridge, whatever you do.   Don't
> trust the* White Mice.

The brass came off the collar; the edge came
off the thirst for beer and complient *Co.*

In-country famfire was an afternoon's drive
to the 'burbs: water buffalo, bamboo, blank stares.
After the requisite 7.62 mm sprayfest, grab-assing
and assured of victory, we boarded the trucks
for Tan Son Nhut.

Far from interstates the backing six-by
knocked down a bamboo shanty, edged away
with blue smoke belching
while two clichéd crones screamed
unheard over the engine's roar.

The driver, a youth of suspect passions,
was laughing, punctuating
the air with fistly emphasis
— *Look what I've done to win the war!* —
and in his second effort
to change direction, caught
in his own myopic self-delusion,
drove over the child.

## Pastorale

Creeper vines
the envy of a celluloid Tarzan
drape blossoms like Spanish tile poppies.
Wild orchids flourish in unlikely settings,
defy arboreal patterns.

Cries of gaudy birds
not quite hidden in the canopy
pull wary eyes toward palm fronds that sway
where there is no breeze.

The jungle,
asserting its territorial prerogatives,
reclaims its own after an hiatus
of village encroachment:
Stones grown under a flourish of bougainvillaea,
the roof poles have begun already to rot;
new maps display no pink at this juncture . . .

The 173rd has worked this province.

## A Transparency Of Seasons

Behind a wall of restraint I watch
a gray shadow watching, patterned
after other shadows,
the measured growth of tulips,
orderly rowed, ranked
columned by function.

Reaching for the blossoms, pulpy
in their brilliant odorlessness, the fiery burst
of color in my hand blots upon the wall.   The stalks
chopped off at the neck or burst
from within under concussion run
red over the mottled green
foliage and laced roots.

> *Somewhere beneath the canopy of*
> *palm and mangrove west of War Zone C*
> *in the back water of conflict*
> *a lone survivor lies in a field*
> *of harvested soldiers, a place apart by reason*
> *of the express focus on concentrated dying.*
> *Alive,*
> *he is out of place . . . but not far.*

*They come for him with stained litters*
*field dressings, rubber-tubed bottles*
*saline for the shock*
*but he confounds them*
*by his unmarked state,*
*comments only on the orderly*
*blossoms in the trees where his eyes stare ...*
*and they look and ignore him when they see*
*the air bursts have rained down all*
*the flowering garnish*
*onto this glade of sorrow.*

Watching with me
the blue-green observer behind
the wall scowls with mild severity:
the blossoms have not been touched —
have grown again — and he smiles and is watched.

Through the walls sounds
are filtered until distant cries come faintly:
keening birds on an April fancy,
a game bidden on some chaotic playground

out of sight, played
under disparate rules, empty
in its inevitable conflict, he hears
the children fleeing the field.
hears their feet pounding the dirt
hears their screams through the louder whining —
the crashing statement of the game wrecker.

The watcher reaches through the wall, springing
aside the bamboo.   It gives easily
and returns after passage.

> *. . . hell, lieutenant, there ain't a mark on
> him. I get a heartbeat.   What is it . . . shell shock?*

The watcher smiles: the flowers spread their sickly
carpet across the width of the field.

> *Ain't no such, no more.   Bag 'em!   Zipper 'em!
> Don't ask questions.   Close his eyes.*

They overtake the road, the field growing outsize.
It disappears beneath a spread
of tiny brilliant bursts of color.
He feels the walls grow
greener, translucent, expanding
he feels the metal coarseness, channeled
non-skid floor
through counter-pulsing percussion giant
blades overhead, feels the room lifting
and the jungle wall melts and drips
away into a receptacle for the destitution of blossoms.

Through the stone, flowers lie where they fall:
blossoms crushed and missing,
stalks shattered.   Sad they are
not perennials.

Walls crumbling,
littered walls receding into green walls beyond,
a serrated progression of walls, staggered,
all falling in screaming silence,
a conspiracy of flowers going to dust,
their time at hand.

## Another Kind Of Understanding

In the Land of the Morning Calm
in another time, another war
they used to say,

>    *He's gone Asiatic!*
>       — a ten-thousand meter stare
>          in a ten foot bunker —

It was the same, though
in the elephant grass
and beneath the triple canopy
where the horizon could be touched
with either hand.

> "The refugees set fire to their small boats as they
> abandoned them, so fires dotted the water at night.
> It was eerie, but it was beautiful.   Cecil B. DeMille
> should have been there."
> — *The Washington Star*, January 1, 1978 —

## Burning Bridges

Nguyen Ngoc Loan,
his aged mother, his wife
and three children (one with dengué) have
beached their fishing boat on semi-hostile shores.
Looking on the ashes of the thrice-functional craft,
they sense the magnitude of their irreversible
Homeric act.
The oblique threat of an unknown future
promises more
than the assurance of a return trip.

The Street of Flowers,
Tu Do, Tran Hung Dao,
no longer policed by the benevolent
incompetence of White Mice
are shooting galleries after dark for errant walkers;
erring talkers vanish in re-education camps.
Cholon has lost
its bamboo-edged Oriental delicacy.

Nguyen Ngoc Loan watches beacon smoke
climb to the clouds hanging above
the muddy waters of the Chao Phraya,
the child with fever
whimpers in pathetic slumber.

**How to Counsel a Real Live Sonuvabitch Second Lieutenant Who Would Seek A Silver Star on a Body Count of Grunts Sent Only to Care For Him**

Frag 'im!

## Man In The Middle

Hawk-eyed hungry
Production lines hum their keening theme:
*First to fight!*
A light sweat beads their sentiments
while they arm the world.

Free-dom has strings.
Their mercenaries by fiat
committed a debt inherited.   Words
serve to stir their ire
until their bunkmates begin to die ...
In the middle.

Ascetic so he looks like a believer;
starry-eyed, their minds dewey with new morning
ideals, rag-tag vestments as much a badge
as the backward look
of their Canadian-bound brothers:
*Hell no!   We won't go!*
And they don't.

Their surrogates queueing in outraged humility
raising quick hands of confidence —
the assurance of youth.
They will need more than slogans
In the middle.

Classroom for a generation;
reduced by polarization and demands,
the class is smaller.

The teaching here is over;
Now the learning begins.
And the man in the middle
finds reason both ways —
neither way.

Those who volunteered his services
buy stock in Arabian oil,
blue chip easements,
still not learning history.

The ones who urged him to stay are forty now,
protesting urban taxes and wondering
if they did right By Madelyn Murray O'Hair.

## Credit Cards And Causes

There you sit in sunback dress
beach tan
and cleavage I don't remember in a skinny sister,
your awkward handling of divided loyalties
obvious,
devouring my coming-home cake with relish.

*Peace Movement!*
you mouth around crumbs
explaining away your growing up
with that transient sanctity of youth and bigotry.

You ask about Cajun Jacques Breaux,
the star of my letters,
and while I try describing how he lies
still
somewhere in the A-Shau
and Sergeants Three
at Xuan Loc, Dak To
and one back in Arlington,
you tell me
about the causes you're into now.

# Grenade

## I

Maybe he was out too long
on long range patrol
scuffling through someone else's real estate.
Maybe

his head heat scrambled
in the oven of APC,
the frying pan of helmet;
or the torque of never-ceasing sound
louder than sound,
and the taste of blood
from lips bitten sometime under concussion —
that could have done a job on him.

Encore rotor failures on shakey frail machines,
invitation to one-way rides.
Too many Eagle Flights even that returned,
that too could have done it.
Going and coming is incidental
and maintains the myth.
Having to go is what garbles the mind.

*Spic, honkie, kike, nigger*
   Manuel, Joe, Abie, Sam
was reason alone.

Or a *Dear John,*
an ignorant southern lout sergeant,
or some career-fearful wearer of brass
who offered them in sacrifice.

The face lost,
the answer lies in scattered remnants of the body.
His duffel bag sat hours later, unclaimed
on the floor of the terminal port,
boarding tag conspicuously clean
with California promise, bright with disuse.
His weapon never turned up.

The guards on the chopper ramp felt the
concussion,
thought it was sappers.
They fired three flares and half a belt of M-60
ruining their night vision.

## II

It was some three hours later
when crew chiefs were clearing
gunships for morning strikes —
and this after they knew who but not why —
that *Tango Quebec Seven*'s copilot
found part of one hand, threatening
but aimless,
thrust into the control panel of the Huey,
the shiny tight completeness of the pin ring
anchored securely beyond the second finger's
second joint.

Part of a jungle fatigue jacket plastered
with dark jelly
to the front wall of the new PX,
the division patch
— two A's back to back —
shredded down to one.

A *Zip* private
doing stockade time for AWOL
washed it off.   Lines
forming for the movie
speculated on the damp blot in the road
and bitched about the heat.

# Mayday!

*Squawk!*
One-five-one is down
beyond Tay Ninh
near a land called Parrot's Beak.

J. C. and Pancho's pilot
out of the blue to blend with the rubber trees
and an ordered forest
that never knew dogwood.

Held upright, revolutionary style
between diminutive weaponed hands,
their Calvary will be the alien sanctuary
of Cambodia

Unless they're lucky
and died in the crash.

We'll know in three days.

## Street Of Hondas

In the *Paris of the Orient* trades were zoned in lots:
One city block marketed only bread,
another blue flowering china of questionable
origin; the next footwear — sandals, black-market-
nylon-webbed-cleat-soled-G.I. jungle boots, and
Parisian pumps for *cheongsam*ed
young girls delicately called *Co.*

The Renault taxi by its own will
slowed along the ranks of bargain bicycles
and threatened to stop
at the display of Hondas in ice cream colors
as if it sought an Asian cousin.   We drove
on to the Rue Catinat but the driver and I,
each with his own visions,
called the eccentric street after the motorbikes.

The streets narrowed through ash,
forges glowing under bamboo sheds.
In the block after labored the coffin makers,
honored in their sweat and forethought
and the frail, fawn-colored boxes displayed
in a range of sizes.

The wall lockers crafted by these artisans all
sprang apart from the heat of the drying lights
against the green mahogany that summer.
They collapsed at night
when souls were most susceptible
to influences, prophetic
as tea leaves and animal entrails.

The craftsman, pressed for his wares,
made no guarantees.   As with the coffins
who would know the uncured state of the box
when it was settled finally, quickly, in the earth.

On that drive the passenger urged the cabman on,
a driver who was Chinese, born in Cholon.
But I keep seeing coffins explode beneath the soil,
dried and thown apart, surprising as the fiery deaths
in khaki or tiger suit fatigues,
the cheap black cotton.

## Sleight Of Hand

I stood beside Lesco
the Gypsy (his family
had always dabbled in magic)
and listened as he droned
his cabalistic incantations
into the handset to a distant
and willing helpmate.

When the veil of smoke was drawn,
I was astonished to see
he had made the entire village vanish.

Lesco's confidence in
his own art always
amazed me.

## The Judas Tree

Joyce Kilmer chanced his visionary mettle:
a tree, superior to mere scribbling,
chosen to speak a sermon in green.

Observing what I can count of canopies,
from my new-age sanctuary hole,
I find the requisite trio: sometimes
it's rubber then something then mangrove,
other times pine then something then ...

Any combination conspires to sap the light
from this shady glade, transforming it
always to a dripping midnight.

The sentience of rubber trees — anomalies.
We enjoy no return on our money,
only French bookkeepers find profit
in accounting bomb damage
and other assessments.

We are charged seventy-five
dollars per tree damaged or done in
— already having paid once at the rate
of point eighty-seven men per growth —
and we don't get green stamps.

Pines, art
works without Oriental
filigree; banyans, twisting like
the layered intertwinings of tortured minds;
mangroves unmeasurable, but
Kowabunga Ken says they reach more than
two hundred feet.   I'm a long way from
chinaberry and paw-paw, magnolia
and cypress familiars.

It might have been worse,
Sergeant-Major said.   In the Huertgen Forest,
eighty-eight airbursts were merely
primary cause,
extending their effective radius through
the flawed logic of physics, incorporating
tree flesh into their deadly formulations,
adding meter-length evergreen splinters
to good German steel shrapnel
seeking out otherwise tree-loving novices.

It could have been any select of this alien
tangle upon which Judas sought expiation,
mistakenly, by terminal suspension
of himself.   God knows,
I would have hoisted him into
position had I known, merely in exchange
for the privilege of leaving
this magic forest.

## Bodycount

Simple equation that makes the stats look good
satisfies the press,
relieves their anxiety over leaving
the Caravelle during happy hour.

Keeps the general off the colonel's ass,
the colonel off the major's,
the major off mine:

*If it's Vietnamese and it's dead . . .*

*it's Viet Cong!*

# The Paddy

Myriad worlds hang in algaeic suspension,
a muddy green universe
of minutiae and men trapped
in obscurity.   Flouting Graham Greene
nostalgia for balmy tropical eves,
an indifferent moon sucks
the heat from these aqueous beds,
drawing out hope with comfort
at an exponential rate.   Climbing,

the lunar floodlight spreads its spectrum
broad across the placid surface,
reaching insistently back
toward aberrant crouching bodies.

Pulpy spring rice shoots,
sinuous and threatening
like tiny kelp strands, are fleshy and clinging
on legs numb from inactivity
and the insidious fall of mercury.
Nearing absolute zero and immobile,
I cringe yet from the touch.   But disgust
has no place in killing and dying.
Aversion to caliginous sensations is newfound.

Once, munching C's sitting on a body bag
was common fare.   Now
the choice between hidden threats
and the assurance of *Charlemagne le Vainquerer*
creates indecision.   Roll call
here is an exercise in necrology.

The water is still around us: nothing moves
but the tiny Asian pests.   They breed here,
live and hunt here,
hanging now in whining saturation
of the motionless air, holding
over sodden warriors a yellow sweating sickness.

A froth of boo waste scum along the dike edge:
ammoniatic vapors rising cloyingly from the murky
surface reinforce suspicions
that this pond, far from farm country,
is not all that unfamiliar.

Bits of crusted fecal matter —
more loathsome for their origin with my own
species — eddy slowly 'round my chest.
An urge to paddle away the filth diminishes
with the obvious growing immobility of my hands.
I dare not splash.

The dike is baked to imporosity,
packed by the scuffling passage of countless
tire-sandaled Annamite feet.

The sloping wet-clay-slick bank against my cheek
smells moldy and rich, not offensive.   Promising
with expectation of growth and nourishment
and cover.

A colony of rats,
resident in an adjacent hedgerow,
waters at this repulsive fountain.
One bold bastard scampers over my hand
and before my conscious will can control it
my reflexes cause tiny
                                        concentric
                    *tiny*
                              *concentric*
circles
out across the paddy.   Hatin' Harry stares
with undisguised horror
at my indiscretion . . . gross inattention.
The rectangular cesspool is not disgusting to Harry,
as it is not to the rats.
They share common concerns.

Neither is it distasteful to the farmer
who pushed the young, apple-green shoots
into the muck of the bottom, filled with
generations
compounded of waste, rotted rice stalks,
and suicidal rats from the hedges.
For the farmer it means life.
For me too . . .
Hatin' Harry, Crazy Bruce and the others.

If the gunships come in the morning
before Charlie — even the *Jolly Greens*
don't venture into the Fishhook
at night anymore — we may yet
make it out of this festering sinkhole,
this Godsend, this oversized
California backyard pool of a foxhole.

When we go into standdown,
I'll remember this paddy with fondness.

# Lord, Praying

This unaccustomed pose,
on my knees among sandbags,
feels counter-productive;
doesn't it say in the Bible, The Lord helps
him who helps himself?    Crouching, thus,
asking for such high-order intervention, flies
in the face of that droll commentary.

And uncomfortable as hell,
the concussion-ordered chaff of
shattered trees, broken branches and pulped
bamboo laced with shards of still-smoldering
metal from incoming,
cuts unevenly through tired jungle fatigues,
lacerates tender body parts.

You and me, God ... right?
I know you've got my six,
and every other azimuth on the clock face,
so ...   break time past,
it's Up and Over,
back earning my keep!

### Gate Nr. 2—TSN

Paddies without grain
surround the Sixty-ninth Signal; pertaining
to the conceit, they breed their own mosquitoes.
Sewage stands in open *benjo* ditches
before the gate: Tan Son Nhut is questionable
shelter.

Beyond the cantilevered concrete and steel
baffle of gate number two,
Fun City, Southeast Asia begins . . .

Downtown Viet Nam is no surprise
but shame cannot be modified by tiny
jasmine garlands
thrust insistently forth from urchin paws, empty.
Hundred-P Alley is a lie; whores
cost more than 100p now.
In Democracy, inflation is allowed.

Blue and cream Renaults
quick land-locked metaled water bugs
scurry frienziedly for GI scrip.
Mama-san will cry when the rate changes:
still, for now, hoarding is a virtue.

Shacks angled crazily against shacks,
Schlitz tin siding
Black Label roofing
standing water and muck beneath the gapped
metal overhang.   Charcoal smoke

*nuoc mam*
and the acrid reek of urine
hangs a rancid curtain across the face
of every cubicle.   Opting for the brunette —
and there are no others —
the bargain is concluded behind clumsily hung
sheets where the children watch: on-the-job
training.

Glittering mirrored bar backs,
neon walls, acid rock ceilings,
every bar a sameness with every other.
Barber shops
where unskilled artisans handclip unwilling white
sidewalls.   Across the road, sandbags and
concertina, deceptive,
fail to protect the insignificance
of the Dustoff pad . . . seldom
does the flurry settle completely.

Newport!   Not a beach:
no whitecaps, no yachts, no tailored lawns,
sculptered statuary.
A tired joke for junior officers.
Its seven-tiered existence is marginal,
its status reviewed daily in the subterranean
halls of COSVN where nightly mortar targets are
fashioned.   Third Field
Hospital, austere in its new role,
where in a shadow of books and desks
displaced colonial dependents struggled
with English verbs

in a French culture
in an Annamite city
in an Oriental world.
Now the stark white eminence harbors
fiercer lessons.

Circle Thirty-four Mess: salads cost extra
movies on Monday and Thursday
strippers on Wednesday and Saturday, God
on Sunday.   Tuesdays and Fridays are quiet.
The salads are better then,
and I went back to see *Dr. Zhivago*
three times in the same week.

BOQ Number One, where salads go with the entree,
but there's never ice for the tea.
Capitolism is failing.

Around the corner
Kong Ly points its promising boulevardness
in palm-lined prominence toward
the Paris of the Orient,
a *chevalier* of streets
paralleling Plantation Road, subtler
in its threat, eminently more scenic.
The rates are higher traveling Plantation:
the Cong work there without regard
to urban renewal.   They believe
re-education will handle that.

## In-bound: Bien Hoa

It is not easy to stand thus
exhibiting some semblance of military bearing,
that martial quality leached out of us
in IV Corp's leisurely canal country,
bled out in field hospitals and *Dust Off*
choppers, blown away in orderly rubber tree
groves the declining French fortunes
still prefer to call plantations,
chastened to commonplaceness in *Tet*, made
news-meaningless by media star tantrums.

Only a milepost marked "Departure"
keeps my focus, the line moving slowly
toward the realm of peaceable kingdoms
and knights of purpose,
the land of round eyes and round doorknobs,
*The World!* But the wide-eyed incoming
shuffle is worthy of note.

This sad procession, despite how it sees
itself, this stream of bright warrior children
jostling their eager way into hell,
griping already about the heat, though
it's early morn yet,
noting with curiosity the tiny peoples
who form the crowds here,

but they turn aside when their vision encounters
our burnt-out eyes, our scarecrow shapes,
our skeletal and atabined skin pale from recent
recovery wards
in ragged, bleached fatigues and boonie hats.

And as their FNG minds grapple with
these unwelcome visions, we play that Devil's
game, a cynical version of choose-up-sides.

Eenie ...
  *Which of this innocent assembly will*
    *return in anonymous aluminum boxes,*
      *their reservations already confirmed at Dover?*

Meenie ...
  *Which missing legs, feet, arms*
    *or eyes, the means or inclination to procreate,*
  *the brain to function returning perhaps in time,*
  *reluctantly, their embarrassment obvious.*

Minie ...
  *Which will vanish into the nowhere*
  *of M.I.A. reportage or P.O.W. vocations.*

Moe ...
  *Which the ones who will, as we do now,*
  *climb these gallows steps returning*
  *in whole or in part to the sentence*
  *of living with all this,*

I hereby bequeath these mere statistics.

## Tracks

In the dripping rainforest and later
in the Michelin groves
drivers say their vision in an APC was zero.
The iron-bound slot on the faceplate
shields III Corps commuters
but tourists and Sunday drivers would
hardly select this behemoth for joyriding.

The lever-loving corporal, oblivious
to the mascot
dashing between the moving column
of iron,
targeted him . . . or ignored him.
Immaterial!

Tropic Lightning was buying
rubber trees: one hundred seventy-five
dollars, and three point seven men per tree.

The dog was not a viable concern.
The thunderous snake of vehicles,
intent on their pancaking parody,
neglected the brief initial yelp.

When the brigade had passed
Gook was part of the landscape
and the cleated belts carried bloody mud
and hair on toward Tay Ninh City.
No one collects GI insurance on pets.

In the Ninth Army's dash through Normandy
behind Blood and Guts
at a road junction near St. Lô
an errant foot soldier made the same dare.
The Shermans of that generation
were scarcely heavier than personnel carriers now,
but after the third tank
the prostrate spreading caricature
melded into the hurried mud of wartime France.

There was nothing to bury,
nothing to send home,
no time to do either.

Tracks ain't nothing to fuck with.

## Confusing Salvation for Absolution

*Yea, though I walk through the valley —*

Tight blue gabardine at twelve, pubescent
sweat deodorant free
shiny last winter's shoes.
After the hymns of thanksgiving
and plate passing . . .
First memories of leaded glass.

*— of the shadow of death —*

Carrot and stick lessons from fanatics:
one eternal bliss,
the other cynical horror.

*— I will fear no evil —*

First cousin to Captain America
turning wine to water behind the shield
fearing the heavenly bolt
when "Bad Ass" sings itself through my devotions,
the hush of sermon pause

*— for I am the meanest sonuvabitch in the valley!*

Reveling in this blasphemous seneschal's
presumption after a hiatus of earthiness,
I am easily swayed.   Watching
Hayes torch a hooch, zapping *Zips*
when they flee the flames, I can believe
again.   My faith is real in the real
lonely though it is
in the valley.

## Point Of View,   Unchanged

The dreams that used to fill my nights —
B movie reruns peopled with grainy images
of stereotype enemies —
of the last bad days
when there were faces,
always quinine-shaded and confident,
faces I could not identify
and children lay scattered dead
in villages that did not exist.

Now I still have dreams
but they are not mine too and
the foreigners in them are not assured,
no sense of evil in their eyes
only myself at the center, and still
villages I think now I know
and the children dead.

## Coming Home

I remember the first time he went away,
To a summer camp in a distant place;
His mother naturally tried to stay
His lust — just one more year of grace!

We laughed at all her brooding fears
And calmed and teased her to consent,
For he was a man despite his young years;
We decided then it was time he went.

We watched him go, adventure obsessed,
His mother's torment unmatched in him.
He fled the place where he'd been blessed,
An anxious scene though hardly grim.

That first summertime was ages long,
The second such season, not even a year.
Time made it easier for us to be strong
Still finding it lonely without him here.

The years grew shorter as he grew to size,
Boy Scouts and college — proud reasons to go;
Then training for soldiering, a dubious prize
Traversed those times and challenged him so.

We saw him off, as chastened he flew,
A chilling day — more bluster than tears —
Away to the war all, believers few,
Trying hard to hide his sorrow, his fears.

The letters were respites, though scarce and short,
Well-chosen phrases providing few clues.
They stopped!   Strange . . . he wasn't the sort
To leaven our loneliness, hiding the news.

Now, finally the anguish of parting is o'er,
The plane taxis slowly, I dread that it's come;
A bunting-draped box appears in the door,
Our son, a statistic, at last has come home.

---

[A note here may be in order as this more conventional
rhymed and verse-delineated piece obviously doesn't resonate
with my usual style of un-rhymed, mixed form poetry.   Even
though it was the old New England curmudgeon and favorite,
Robert Frost, who said, "Poetry without a rhyming scheme is
like playing tennis without a net." (sic), my poetry has only
worked for me in that more modern, unformatted vein.   This
poem resulted from a grad-school-assigned exercise in, I think
Engl 571 (Poetry), paying homage no doubt to the now-
distant purveyors of line, rhyme, capitalized first words and a
paucity of punctuation.   An anomaly?   Just skip over it, next
time you make a passage through this little volume.//RJF]

### Aix-en-Provence, April '70

*Regardez vous Indo-Chine!*
Blood red script on the metro wall
competes with enticements of commercial
appeal.

I wonder we didn't think of that.
Having failed their lessons without
remedial coaching they went on
to greater embarrassment in Algeria.
What are we going on to?

*Rends moi mes morts.*

# Unmarked Falling

Sharp-creased khakis break
over spit-shined glossy leather.
A rubber tipped wooden stave gleams
in the setting sunlight —
the unreconstructed veteran

silently watches a whitewalled corporal
(too young to have shared in this)
perform the mechanical sunset ritual
before the pristine block catafalque.

Down the hill
below the cream mansion, beneath
a mortally blighted maple,
the soldier stands again

before the smaller stone:
a familiar name and number.
The Unknown Soldier is a myth
only in the cold marble.

## Wire

Once as a child on the farm
I tore a berry-stained hand on a rusty talon
of fencing.
Grandma put kerosene on it
      — a very southern remedy —
but my mother insisted . . .
I cried when I got the shot.

Flat crowned and ten-gallon-hatted outriders,
myth building down the years,
stretched long shimmering bands of
two prong and Glidden strands
across the land
along the steady flowing east-west highways.

On the docks at First Log
ugly rolls with hotcross ends
share the Sea-Land space with
pallets of Lucky Lager
      stacks of C's
         empty aluminum boxes.

At Phan Thiet astride Route 13
on a hill that bears the name of its prominence
      *Four-sixty-seven*
the sun creeps up, scattering demons
beyond Phan Rang,
somewhere in the 101st's area of operations.

The colonel told me Apollo works
for the Screaming Eagle.

Here the wire,
concertina in stark prickly relief
against the blaze of dawn,
is strung with rags and odd, disjointed puppets
no longer responsive to strings.

Tiny brown commissars who came last night
without invite, must stay now
indifferently awaiting the cleanup squad.

The hot season is months away,
the heat of the day hours distant, yet
already yesterday's *nuoc mam* and garlic are
blending gasses
in the few bellies that are whole,
filling the dawn with a wretchedness
only scavengers can cure.

The wire will be clean before dark,
long before they come again,
but already the enthusiasm for windchimes
is waning.

## Swampdusk

Ghosting by, water tangent
and proximate, swooping,
I can't tell loon from bittern

their cries too similar:
both vanish, lured
from a placid life.

The Loaches looked like that
and the Hueys
when we came back across
the mythical border
out of the Kingdom of Kampuchea.
*Cambodia*, the Ops order read.

Afraid of what I'll catch — a vanity
cascading with time — I cannot
fish these waters again,
not since the rains came.

## An Every-Other-Day Kinda' Thing

Jeep-shaped hearse
crawling over bleached concrete apron,
metal surfaces
soaking reflected heat through
already sweat-dark flight
suits.   Stifling . . .
line crew shirtless, dripping
on
        under
                by the earth-
bound craft like brown and green, great
shiny silver-eyed maggots, feeding on the odd
aluminum carcass.

Under the wing smells are different: in the heat
is sterile nothingness, slightly
musty, of hot white sand
burnt oil
salt air
JP-4 fumes rising
in nauseous shimmering waves
to distort the tranquil bay
beyond.   Here meager shade evokes
an odor of mold, space and cold clouds
above, then is hastened away
by the arid eruption of rancerous winds,
yields to drifting stench — Vietnamese
fishing village:
garbage dead fish feces on the tide.

Cowl flaps replaced, slammed
shut, buttoned up.
Eyes bottomless and inward
reflect only *time*,
less *time*,
less and less *time*.

Anonymous call for crew check rapid voices:
Chute harness —
     (Chute's in the aircraft)      *Check!*
Water wings —
     *Check!*
Radio beeper —
     *Check!*
Weapon —
     *Check!*
Ammo —
     *Check!*
Smoke grenades —
     *Check!*
Currency stash —
     (Piastres, francs, $50 bill)      *Check!*
Survival kit —
     *Check!*
Knife —
     *Check!*
Coffee cannisters —
     *Check!*
Water cannisters —
     *Check!*

Galley rations —
> *Check!*

Blood chits —
> (worth a fortune to a Zip whether he brings
> you in alive or dead: it's your ass they pay
> for, not your life.)
>> *Check!*


Three pilots, pre-flight
complete, flip for two seats.   Loser sleeps
going out.   He doesn't smile.   It means
two night landings, one night takeoff coming
back.   You play the cards you're dealt.

With flight imminent discomfort
in the heat fades.   It's better here than aloft
far to the north.   Hold to this blistered,
pockmarked land.   Stomachs tighten — sphincters,
too, hopefully.   The GIs are bad on the ground, but
Sweet Jesus
in the fearful sky. . . .

No chance for abort, two miserable
grave-robbing mechs smile assuringly.
And if they scratch today, it's up on the board
again for tomorrow.

Gear in . . . crew in
minus engine-start fire watches standing
aft the huge props.   Extinguishers primed,
generator gearing down, loading . . .
throat-deep chuckle

*cough*

phlegmy snort of blue smoke
trails back
from where the prop rested.

One!

Number two snarls,
belches . . . catches . . . dies.   Switch off, switch on.
Winds
and winds
        and winds
                and winds
                        and winds and *coughs* . . .
catches.   Holds
erratically, then steadies and
settles into pace with number one.

Needles quiver in synch.
Gauges flicker in spasm, level off in turn.

Two!

Service disconnects, draws rapidly
away, two cherry-flame
bottles flung on top.

Up
between paired flashing four-blade knives.
Up
through hanging wheelwell doors, quickly
Up
into the gloomy maze, the mechanical, bomb bay
doors, stowing
      locking
      belting
            checking . . .
a scheduled pace, a ballet
never quite in time with the music.

Heat trapped in the standing plane
eats at rationed energies.  Blowers
can do only so much as the beast
is resurrected, flings off the maggots
who seek the next carcass on line,
reluctantly lumbers across crackle-plate ramp
like a giant rusty water buffalo.

*Taxi* . . .
      power checks
      clear, lock guns
      sweat.
*Taxi* . . .
      intercom checks
      auxiliary generator check
      verify chute pull-away racks.
*Taxi* . . .
      stifling, dripping bodies packed
      too tight in odorous confinement

in ditching stations, strapped in seats
against bulkheads, crowding the floor.
Sweat.

*Taxi* . . .
wingtips bouncing, Neptune belly undulating over
sand-washed taxiway troughs, varicam clanking
disastrously, flaps grinding out, then back in
spastic,
jerking.

*Taxi* . . .

*Jesus, God!   Where's the end of this bitchin' strip?*

Brake check, bodies
straining forward against retaining straps, braces,
rolling again.

*Taxi* . . .
and sweat
all the length of the sand- and wind-scoured
concrete path to the terminal ramp;
line up behind a VNAF flight,
an aged camouflaged derelict from wars gone
by.   A once-honorable Charlie-Four-Seven,
now saturated with the stench
of unwashed bodies and puke and dried blood and
pig shit and urine and *nuoc mam,*
the fish sauce minimizing all else.

Ancient mariner of this jungled kingdom
forced to wander the hostile skies
forever, seeking permission to land:
beset, as with scurvy — it radiates an aura
of shame and disgust with its own
downfallen state.   Ahead

a Pan-Am R-and-R flight,
sleek, clean charter.
They go to Hawaii: we go to Eye Corps,
the Ashau, a night landing-takeoff at Da Nang
with the strip under fire.

They go to tumble sweat-sweet wives,
passioned ravages in aching love beds.
We go to get screwed over Khe Sanh.   It's easy
to forget how many days since we surfed
the white linen sheets of Waikiki.

Aircraft swings and backs,
engines run up as the C-47 clears.   Next ...

Jet start!   One screaming whine follows
the other, clean smooth.   No pulse-seeking
hopes like with the recips.   Though
eardrums protest with ringing clarity
and dual screeches proclaim loss of the
last hope of abort, it comforts.   No time to savor
the dichotomy

— a rolling start,
turning on the run into the furnace wind
knotted belly as
roll
     turns to
         leap
             turns to
                flight.

Climbing out
banking clear of the pattern,
clearing Cam Ranh control, every action
now remote, trained for, automatic
through continued climb onto the initial
heading, alert to radio check on Qui Nhon
tower:
     "Garbage***garbage***garbage***
     Cat's Paw four-niner-one***
indecipherable bullshit" crackles
on the ethereal waves, heavenly wrinkled plastic
frosted with the hidden tracking
stars overhead.   On freq . . . up tight!   So
back into drifting nowhere for an hour.

Opal skitches of sand
washed by the South China Sea flow
brokenly northward.   Unlike
the calculated precision of our passage
this coast is ragged, shaggy trailing feathers of a
vulture's wing ... but it stays
there, a familiar reference beneath
the port wingtip.

Turning on a beacon azimuth
shakes loose the sloth of drifting indolence.
Positions manned, no longer meaningless seats of
passengers.
These ticketed flyers come to bring hurt.

A Marine Phantom appears, too close —
with Peter Pan mystique, pilot's thumb
up like a beaming Nero.   Then, the hurt.
Hammered blazing projectiles
arc harmlessly away toward the receding
water in check fire: How many fish have we
killed with this block-checking?

Beneath, muddy quicksilver river meanders
aimlessly, green whorling steppes
and tangled jungle blanket the real world
down there somewhere.   Ahead
a jumble of rocks runs into boulders,
up into rearing hills, and are lost finally where
whitecaps of fleece break slowly
over craggy, mortar-scarred peaks.

Powerplants drone through
overpowering sharpness of bleeding fuel.   Unseen
micro-cracks hidden strut, aluminum
skin wrinkles minutely.   A giant hand tweaks the
bird's tail, undiscovered
beneath the muscle-spasming slam
of the varicam.   Tracking a grid line trail,
a vector without start, without
finish, up the river,

indecision at the confluence
beware the border: beyond there
the world is flat
and my little ship will fall off.   Columbus
you bastard — you were wrong!

Turbulence from a clear sky: beautiful, awesome,
that same F-4 drops past at two o'clock, a Foucault
suspension that rotates
within its world nine thousand feet below, falls as
an arrow from a destructive bow in the sky, then
squirts heavenward from a homemade hell of
napalm and high explosive.

> *"Will ya' ook at that!   Zang*
> *spat in the target area, some*
> *little Charlie bastard*
> *had the balls to open fire . . ."*

reaching insistently, impotently up, with
a chatter unheard.   F-4's wingman does not admire
him, unloads his ordnance on some little Charlie
Bastard (who) had the . . .

A private war, it fades behind, silent
in its intensity, unheard above the engines.
Performed with the repetitious inevitability
of the last great (*sic*) personal war, and
the one before . . . and the one before that,
> *ad initium*
> *ad interum*
> *ad finem!*

From the burnished bronze wall ahead through the
Plexiglas, three refracted suns sink: quicksilver

    becomes tarnished lead
        becomes pebbled green carpet
            stretching into black nothing.


Climb!
Above the night-shrouded peaks;
clearance is the only reality.


Ten thou' five and up, climbing.   Raw
musky smell of rubber mask, pure oxygen startles
the lungs.   Fumes belabor smarting eyes.
Screaming popping surges of twin power overlie
a muffled cacophany of constrained voices
that cannot be heard.


On around the giant circles and ovals,
figure eights,
        lines
            boxes,
                S-turns for variety.
No creeping trail; no crawling convoys
not spoken for — no night sounds on the river
not made by rightful inhabitants, so . . .
still the guns . . . hold the flares — a while.   With
the night will come fear below
in the hamlets, in the foxholes
the bunkers still wet with seasonal
overabundance;

chopper pads hacked out of a jungled denseness,
firebases of tenuous and marginal residency.

Hang in there over the Ashau.
Khe Sanh deceptively still, waiting
'til mortar rounds come walking with giant
blasting steps, a monstrous, vengeful puppet
on strings pulled by tiny brown men
and women
and children.

Squealing across the band, Fox Mike
is heavy with chatter:
    *"Fire mission . . ."*
artillery FDC calls a ground spotter
who will never answer.   Perimeter
head count, patrol check-ins:
    *"Request — URGENT — Dustoff"*
and some leg outfit near Quang Tri calls
for Puff, the Magic Dragon.
Too far to share our benevolent intentions,
too near not to bring sweat.
Chopper flight chatter . . .
ground control sweet-talking a FAC
along the DMZ, down in his devotion.
Poor timing!

Dark suffuses the land,
hides the downed pilot, but it hides
too, the night-flowering adversary, outlines
in exhaust ports, control
panel lights, Jolly Greens who might come

seeking, grateful for his devotion,
and if Charlie heard him, it's odds-on
they have him spotted.

Inscrutable (read blank) faces wait patiently for the
Big Mamas to *Whop! Whop!* their embracing
safety onto the hilltop. But they come anyhow.

Fireflies below, winking wickedly as we pass,
rising become drifting orange basketballs,
arcing away from our wracking, life-saving turn.
Greasy black and grey flowers of fear
blossom out red-orange in the night sky,
seeking
reaching along the abandoned path, their seed
pelting the ridiculously thin skin like angry rain.

Hold, in the turn! Through
the edge of the somber garden, untended,
only sky, devoid of threat beyond
being intimidated to death.
No fire! No leaks! No blood.
No more!

Back on track
droning,
waiting,
searching, traversing the squealing bands.

Smell of greasy rations
from modern America's dream
kitchen galley over stench

of sour, fear-flooded sweat, cramped fug.
Prop pitch changes: sharper roar,
a difference soon fading
to anonymity in its familiar dissonance.

Necks stiffen, stomachs
quease, joints ache.   Spectral voices speak
on invisible electrical strings
where there are no voices, only
wind-trailing silence.
Our self-conscious parade
the object of ten thousand almond
eyes along the unseen hill line,
paralleling the reaching mountains.

Thunderheads —
                three miles straight up —
Wodin's castles in blue, black and silver clods,
impassive pylon to turn on
following a course change, diverting
to a new track.   And well so:
on an earthly plane ahead a cauldron
of boiling earth — fiery, roiling earth — spills
over, upward, a sheeted wall
of blasting destruction rearing itself.   Unseen
in the starless lampblack void above
the heavy bombers plow unfeelingly on.
Having blindly wreaked their vengeance
by radared hands, passionless they retire
to crusty land masses in the distant Pacific and
less hazardous pastimes,
less demanding exercises,

drawing not on the body's sap for daily
rations of hate and acquiescence.

Cynical eyes look down,
follow the fires, neither delighted nor saddened
at the deaths brought by friends
to enemies
for the sake of —

Cynical
comes easier than compassionate:
taxes are up, unemployment's up, youth's up.
No way to stay the mind
when relief to eat means relief
from responsibility for all that happens below,
diminished obligation to think on business at hand.
No prepared channels controlling errant thoughts.

Delicious eroticisms taunt us
in our spatial suspension,
of lonely, hungry wives . . . wet smiles between
long sleek legs . . . breasts swollen from neglect,
hardened quivering nipples . . . tastes . . . scents of
sweets mouths hot demanding
arms winding, holding, feeling,
wanting . . .
          not wanting. . . .  Each to his own.

Air Force nurses who give greater meaning to the
term; a Kowloon whore. face dimly remembered
but the body indelible with assumed passion,
worth the fee in Hong Kong dollars.

The Red Cross slut who takes the grunts' combat
pay — sixty-five bucks a crack — the pun
pales with the demands of abstinence,
Sydney *Sheilahs* and Bangkok *Numbah-Wan*
girls: a hundred miles of it in Saigon alone;
nothing but diseased dregs
in the northern coastal towns.

An absurdly calm background call
for *Dustoff!* brings other visions to interrupt
the clinging fantasies of indulgence: long
lo-boy passing on the base perimeter, bed
stacked two deep neatly symetrically with
unmarked aluminum boxes so obvious in their
casual passing; newly orphaned child
standing stork-like on one leg, the other not
folded Oriental style, but torn away in a
tangle of flesh and ligaments and blood
that won't clot, self-consciously trying to stem
the flow of glistening blue-white intestines,
embarrassed, who didn't know he was dead, went
on standing long after the smoke and dust
from the Russian rockets cleared.

Concrete troughs 'round the walls of the field
morgue piled higgledy-piggledy
with earthly remains and earthly does not enter
ionto it: legs and heads, pieces
fingers torsos arms — maniacs sentenced to die in
the work when they refused to die in the field
sort through and puzzle
together the requisite components

to fill one more box and label it
marked: shipped for burial, wet glistening wounds
hasten back the finer images of female solace
where wet gaping wounds are sought after
for release without the blood and bone fragments,
perfumed fragrance trumps real world.

Shatterer of dreams, with a crack and a blast
a ninety-millimeter attention-getter.
A second lesser jar, screaming voice of alternate
giggles confirms a hit, but powerplants
turn sweetly on.   No casualties,
miniscule hydraulic bleeding . . .
a pressure bandage serves.
No casualties — read a newspaper
and get the picture, the Caravelle picture;
but sweat through a mission and know!

Climb,
away from the ninety, calling for suppression.
A Thud, MISTY bird, lost he must be, slides up from
back in the haven of now-friendly darkness,
thumbs his recognition in the dim lime glow
of cockpit across the lunar-lighted gap
of frigid sky, intercoms confirmation of flashes
through the jungle canopy, rolls away,
brings hurt on another Hanoi draftee gun crew.

Command track stable, lower now, in gun range
if they choose to fire, but they observe closely
the lessons on point.   Thanking a merciful being for
arbitrary beneficence.

A million dreams, a thousand dragging heartbeats,
one constant fear later the time is served out,
dictated by fuel-sucking machines:

> *And when the fans stop turning, Clyde,*
> *this mother glides like a greased*
> *footlocker.*

Look back toward the Ashau —
look away, laughing inwardly: suspicions
and fear have fled, as we are fleeing now,
playing tag with a great, haunting almost-was
behind us through the rain and clouds
and umbrella of black.   Reaction weakens
bladders.   Believers are lined before the relief tube.

Buckle in again, *Immediament!*, for the second act
curtain, *Entr' acte, finito!*
Beyond the changing land, dropping to the coast,
eventually a carnival of lights, Christmas-colored
and columnar.   More waiting, circle following, jet
trailing, through a bucking glide,
two turning, two burning,
a long thumping drop, bump, and moonlit,
black-streaked concrete holds us.

Flares hanging circumferentially about the field
cast dancing shadows on passing faces
and choppers, jets and fence posts alike.
The strip is warm, humid, and the incoming
is 'way off there on Marble Mountain — *Sorry on*
*you, Marines!* —

gratefully removed far enough.   Lights
up the side of Monkey Mountain provide
garish targets for anxious little commissars
and make us grateful for each hated flight
that takes us above this.   Living *is* easier with
sickening air pockets, gut-rending air bursts.
An entire existence — life,
love, dreams, children — dependent
upon a proximity fuse.

Kids for pilots, old men for leaders . . . all this
and still, if not better, then cleaner
than grenades and mud and mortars
and *pungii* stakes, and *waiting!*

The waiting down here is worse,
so when the fueling is done and lift-off completed,
forgetful boredom will come quickly,
and sleep follow on the cold channel-riveted
floor panels that carry us dreamily, fitfully back
to do it all over again
come two days hence.

## Counting Days

Numbers that are not just digits
but forevermores, each ticked off
torn out
blue-ink-streaked into nothingness
as they pass.   Creeping
days, lagging
weeks, agonizing
months — eternal year.

Time passes, but not for the silent
the missing
the dead.
Still I wait and count,
for while I live it passes for me.

Planes leap skyward, joyfully.
Ships back seaward,
churning gratefully seaward,
heading east going west
to a mythical land of mists
where life yet holds,
dream worlds apart.

And if dreams be all,
still they're mine, shared
with one in that shadowy haven,
the land of round eyes,
nights without ambush.

Counting days, anxious,
the stray rocket looms
that never threatened before —
errant shell, deadly mortar, hidden mine.
Preciously careful
as if this goal might be reached.

Counting nights, lonely, aching,
from three digits
through two
to singles . . .

and gone.

## Vicarious Hero

I thought all soldiers heroes then
when they came from the war in bloused khaki,
rainbowed in unit patches.
I was still allowed to run barefoot in the summer
dust that year.

I had a cousin — or rather
a man who married my big-breasted cousin — for a
hero, unclaimed by other relatives.
He brought a German officer's dress dagger,
attractive in its cold steel beauty,
repellent with its broken cross
and a pistol which he never let me fire.
He had other evidence then
which I cannot remember now.   It did not impress
me so much as the magnetic tools for killing
and for dress.

I did not know then that some soldiers got rich
selling the chaff of battle,
and some became heroes merely by purchase.
This pseudo-cousin, pseudo-hero was in my mind
last week when the grinning captain
offered to buy some Viet Cong papers
and an AK-47 from me
between Bushmills in the Gunfighter Club
in Da Nang.

Fresh from Quang Tri,
except for airplane drivers, Zoomies
can be excused or ignored for this barefaced
breach of an undefined etiquette.
It is difficult for airdales to pose
as a contact sport participant.
He would only lie
and say a friend of his in the Green
Berets — a real mean sonuvabitch — gave it to him
for imagined deeds.

My supplicant was different.
The Army staff officer from Mac-Vee
wanted to buy a piece of the action,
wanted to homestead in the myth.   He
snarled his disappointment
when he learned I'd turned them over to the intel
weenies.
His image-crafting desire turned
to disgust with bureacracy.

I must be tired.   I said nothing.   The captain
saved his ass that day when he turned away
to eavesdrop on a Jolly Green pilot
fluttering his hands down the sky of the bar
in mournful replica of his loss:
        a sister ship
        a brother pilot.

Or I saved his ass when I said to Mister Kemp,
pushing back from the rail,
        *Let him be, Jack.   He doesn't even know.*

## Residue

All that is left . . . after
macabre fishing voyages in warm waters
where the catch does not come
flopping onto the decks in schools, spilling
from nets silvery-sided and glistening
with fight,
but scramble aboard in desperation, snared
finally from a death of indifference.

Tiled subway wall canvases
where domestic Van Goghs
have blazoned their fear, their mutilation
and confusion across the gaze of trapped
commuters in two-for-one-sale colors.
Grime of passing has not covered bridges
and landmarks:
cries on scapes appear incessant in change.

Bitter comedy in the sightless paraplegic, wheeling
rat-frenziedly through the mazed
corridors in a five-sided building,
untouched by those he would touch
with his plea.

Saturday night
VFW smirks when the latest generation bellies up:
angry old men who have forgotten their fears,
angry young who forget their condemnation,
accept their sentencing in places discarded
in tattered newsprint.   Rhetoric

marks the fading warriors who never vacationed
in the Ia Drang Valley, cannot comprehend
the endless commonplaceness of Tet.

Behind a fringed shade on a side street
in Carbondale, in a weathered shack on a mudflat
outside Pensacola, in a drawing room looking east
across the fog-cushioned summer rocks
of Hampton; in Anaheim and Ashville, in
Milwaukee and Miles City old women wait,
young women grow old with waiting,
believing . . . hoping.

A warrior, stripped
of his shield, funny-eyed with grass and speed,
with the holy word,
with too many incoming rounds,
too many outgoing litters . . .
too young to understand counter policy, waits
on an empty street, pinned in the light
of an unforgiving sun for a parade
that will never start.

The last journalist, looking back on his efforts,
biased by nature and by calling, stands
alone in a market and watches
fish being wrapped in newspaper.   On impulse
he seeks primacy in that chain, will forget
his written words and take up the nets.
He takes his scaly purchase along with his vow
while his eyes continue their search
for tomorrow's by-line.

Poets whose storehouses of anguish force
a crack in the dam of murky truths and lies —
novelists whose time has come,
apologists whose time is gratefully ending, look
to the black-on-white rites for absolution.

The short days and long nights
of rice paddies and jungled trails, of chill
rain-swept mountain galleries and blistering
red dust ambusheries — deaths and lives,
planned or unexplained, and the extraordinary
acts that graced those stages —
are monochrome in intensity.

In the seasonal light of man-made memories
black and white do not exist: nothing there is
so pure.

## Disquietetude

Rock strewn the path — guiding
pavement-trained strides down from the roadway.
Seeking the green-hiding-gray of the stream,
pine needles resin-fresh underfoot —
leads to the big ones.

Brookies,, speckled
flame-streaked here, don't feed on surface bait.
They lurk!   Mad
reason fights the sense of it.

Entering the line of forest below the rifts
something
  everything
slips uneasily into a parallel
      parallel
a word, the transposed warning . . .
*Treeline!*
bracketed with fears out of time.

Stepping ballet-toed with caution
now, shadows deeper than mere shade
as skin pebbles with old awareness,
quivers as a horse shakes off flies.

Eyes, other sensors scanning,
narrowed against the always unseen:
searching out thin strands, leaves
on a path where they would not fall,
too-normal normalcy.
I am as before the predator
not alone in my trade.

The absence of bird sound,
unnoticed but for stillness in the air,
echoes other absences; whip-sawing cicadas
away for the moment are missed;
leaves too rigid find me
anxious toward spare rodent actions.

Emerging through boulders defining the run
watching the swirl of trout-speared current
I live again in sun with the questionable
half-memory of dark boughs past ...
And breathe ...
And forget bargained prayer promises.

Then lofty thunder miles above
trailing unseen in the void
stampedes me back,
awaiting ARC LIGHT
and for my quixotic travels
I am caught in this other self.

## Survivals

November
downside of the year . . .
village streets overhung
with bells that will not ring,
red-berried wreathes that smell of plastic
wrap, tinsel candles,
obscene Santas in styrofoam.

Flamboyant maple
dress in tidy heaps
shadows the base of trees,
swept crisp into pyramids —
fields for burning, gold and red carnage,
lifestyle of the season.

On a branch against the autumn sky
persists one cluster, leaves
not brown
or red or even gold;
green, not yet begun to fade.
An anachronism of verdure
anomalous in its perennial audacity,
flaunting its perverse indestructibility,
it is so alone!

> *The first time, there was wonder,*
> *a curiosity only: a missed meal*
> *and comrades found in the rubble*
> *missed the rest of the war.*

The maples, bare
but for the stubborn aberration, sway
in the preparative winds of coming winter.
Unstrung fletches, green against
the backdrop sky
where a hawk drifts on the airborne tide.

His wings do not flap; neither does he fly,
but slides, whispering
acrest the bitter drafts,
lazing through altitudes haughty in rule
over domains synthetically ordered.

> *The next time I knew an uneasy fear.*
> *Without playing odds, I sat out the*
> *mission and Army One-Five-One took out*
> *three rows of sapping trees*
> *in Michelin Tresieme.*

Out of the west
down from eight o'clock high, like a MiG
hurled at a BUF, a murderous
deranged starling bold
in his madness dives
on the hawk complacent with ignorance.

One slashing pass and the interceptor climbs out,
erratic, a killing urge sated.
The hawk staggers
across the cobalt battleground, flounces,
regains what little remains
of a reigning demeanor.

A feather — hawk or starling — spirals
crimson with stain
through the branches of the maple to blend
in the fire of the fallen leaves.

> *The third time is when the dreams began:*
> *hooch and bunk, rent by Slavic steel,*
> *rotting sandbags against sweating cheek,*
> *aces and queens wasted like the chips*
> *across the abandoned floor,*
> *and the rockets walking away through the*
> *silent aircraft crouching in revetments.*

Faced with anomalies of the maple
and the audacious starling
I can but marvel on this silly season,
acknowledging my own part
in these pompous grasps for survival.

Down the darkened hallway behind me,
away from the militant, feathered avenger,
discounting greenness in the sugared bough,
seeing only irregularity, ugly in the burnished
steel shard against blue velvet,
the memory is overplayed.
How dramatic we posture
over mere instinctive survival.

Probably the hawk would understand.

### Fortunate Brother: An Echo

That echo again:
"I don't know if I died in Vietnam or not ...
yet."
And he had not.
But he did.

Lewis Puller the First,
Marines' Marine.
Standing tall for him was a
long day's work; no way
could I have been his son.

But I saw that small copy,
that echo,
in the not-so-halcyon days of Lejeune.
He knew he had his work
cut out for him.

And then that next war —
one in a series —
called on him to pay
those Marine dues, the standards set
in Haiti, Nicaragua, Shanghai,
the 'Canal, Cape Gloucester, Pelilieu,
Inchon, Koto-ri (the frozen Chosin),
and there was no choice.

The melody of his echo
might have sung itself true
once he found his level.   But
he never had the time.

And to appease the gods of irony
it had to be American goods
that got him.

He died then
in that 105-shaped crucible,
died,
dragging the remnants
along behind him
down all those years.

Making schools, hospitals, courts —
the institutions of blithe conceit —
his world,
wheeling defiantly through the choruses
of conflict, bearing
the woman's gifts:
solicitude, patience, her love.
But he'd died long before.

And when he put the piece to his head
and touched flame to the pain,
it was only the prudent final step.
The closing down,
not dying again.

And those of us who stumble forward,
we were fortunate to have him,
even dead.   He showed us
the dead can speak.

And it wasn't only for Dad,
the Chesty,
but for all his brothers
dead and dying.

## Silent Night, Wary Night

● 1800 hours, 24 Dec 1968: Assumed the duty for (scheduled) CW3 Jackson Spain: OD, Newport BOQ Saigon-TSN.  *Ho!  Ho!  Ho!*

— SP5 Bullock, duty driver, courier, dogsbody
— Signed for 17 asst'd keys on ring; duty weapon .45 cal. semi-auto pistol, mod 1911A-1 (dirty) w/2 mags ball ammo (dirty); one vehicle, believed to be, beneath permanent coating of mud and *Ba-Mui-Ba*, a Jeep, vehicle nr. 66965... (remainder of nr. missing). Locked and loaded.

● 1922: Star in the east.  Quaint cliché.  *Really bright star!*

● 1957: Jingle ... *of sleigh bells?*  Unlikely effusion of seasonal metaphors.  And a red arc at 3K ft (est) across northern sky.  *Rudolph?*

● 2115: Three kings are late; distinct absence of wise men.  *Fantasies!*

— Eastern star vanished, dropped to the ground, small parachute crumpling into prized heap dangling burnt flare in some bamboo thicket; small children will seek it out at first light.
— Sleigh bells: tinkle of spent brass swept from a quasi-DUST OFF/gunship on 3$^{rd}$ Field Hospital's pad. Crew chief nightly scut work.

— Northern red arc erratic; Spooky on a killing spree!  *Merrie, merrie, merrie.*

 (Flying the Fish Hook yesterday, rife with pine trees; got McNew to drop down to enjoy some seasonal greenery.  Substantial groundfire.  Grinch bastards.  But I digress ...)

• 2050: Despite crucially attuned ears, nothing!

• 2138: Duty Sgt, 509$^{th}$ walked in.  Wants help to change a tire, 100P Alley.  *Rii-i-ght!*  No, seriously.

• 2225: 3$^{rd}$ Field Hosp. heli-pad quiet; business down; things looking up.

• 2245: checked Newport bldg; nobody on roof (how odd; MPs live up there), not even the guard overlooking *Herr General's* digs.

 — Alien beings on 4$^{th}$ level.  Smell female ... can't be; this is a male BOQ.  Remains quiet.

• 2310: Shots fired next door/ARVN vehicle park, JGS. Who knows?  No alarm follows.  *Who cares?*

• 2356: Getting close now — I can smell reindeer shit on the balmy Southeast Asian night breeze.

• 0004: Lost my concentration, slipped into Xmas morn fantasy, missed the midnight roll-over.  Best present I can hope for?  Get through a night alive.
 — One at a time.  No sweat.

• 0040: Spanish Jack disembarked a cab at the front door, stiffed the cabbie, and ripped the door off the Renault.   Seems a bit testy.   (I'm doing Christmas duty for Jack in exchange for New Year duty; he took his nurse-woman to a dance/party at the nurses' BOQ.)   Short night for him; must be that time of month for her.

— Still waiting for Santa.   Hope he doesn't show up wearing a cone-shaped bamboo boater.

• 0156: Sky lit up, northeast.   Gotta be Ben Cat. *Sinh Loi.*   Hel-*lo*, American ceasefire.   Apparently learned nothing.   Season's best, you poor buggers.

• 0210: Duty driver's back.   Dog robbers at Circle 34 Mess wouldn't part with so much as a single bacon sandwich.   "They ran out!"   Uh-huh!   Mess cooks' contrived families, bar girls and pimps are eating, no doubt.

• 0246: Cleaned the .45, reassembled it (eventually). *Voila!*   No leftover parts, nothing missing.   What now?   Elves?

• 0320: On another walk-thru pass , brought down family photo album.   The wife and kids — *Don't go there!* he said, entreatingly.

• 0323: Quet.

• 0329: Column raggedy-ass APCs from 25th Inf. Div. came up from Plantation Rd., past BOQ.

— Going where?   Can't go downtown; nobody needs them in Gia Dinh.   Lost!

• 4 o'clock: That's oh four hundred (0400) hrs for you night-stalkers in civilian garb, airdales and other wastes of space.

— Still, if it were colder ... No!   Never mistake this cesspool for the Holy Land.   Nevah hoppen, G.I   .

• 0444: Firing beyond Gen. Abram's qtrs; checked roof; guard where he should be and both front and side guards at post.   All seem OK with gunfire; not disturbed or reacting.   Revelers!   Sleep well, Gen.

• 0522: Sky lightening.   Can't help remembering other Christmas morns: kids clattering down stairs, bright expectant eyes, hair like brush fire, baggy-toed jammies.   Mama looking great, seasonal.

— Heart-breaking visions ... and I look up, there's Kingston.   Hung over.   Scuffling out to catch a ride to the flight line.   Looks like Death's vomit.   I've seen better conditioned bodies cable-dragged behind tracked vehicles.   Enough firepower hanging off his lanky frame to start WWIII.   Now there's an advent calendar picture.

• 0605: Adjutant called; I'm relieved of duty.   Duty weapon, keys and log to head shed with Bullock.

— Officially on Christmas holiday ... for 1 hr, 25 mins. Manifested on first mission flight of this Holy Day, 0730 hrs w/Sky Queen.

Duty tour, CW2 Robert J. Flanagan ends, 0615 hrs, 25 Dec 1968; relieved by Adjutant.   Paraphrasing Saigon Baby Jo-San: *Looky, looky; you be pleasing!*

## On Appreciating the Poetry of Denise Levertov

Deities are to be sat at the feet of,
suppliant noviceship in art;
so I, seduced by popular acclaim, sat thus
and found opposition to be out of vogue
though crying for expression.

But that was craft and not heart —
a choice of hearing music or seeing pictures only
hung in the balance, and times change
whether you will or no.

Accepting the rhythmic modulation
with alacrity, accommodating
to correct, to repair, to satisfy,
obliging in re-make to an older form
fresh images to satisfy fickle art,
I discovered anew that point of view,
which makes the poet
(a thing I already suspected),
must change with the times,
or the scribe languishes in trite moderation,
a voice without an echo.

Reading again as self-tutoring
demands the flowing poetry
that depends so on commonplace
alignment marks and lines, I discovered
in the dust a false freedom
obscured by lovely memories

and predictable emotions and was reminded
that art consists also of truth.
I had found myself on the wrong end
of the kaleidoscope where black is white
and gray not an accepted shade of reality.

You penned the poignant images so diffidently
of footless children in Thai Binh (Peace) Province,
and children in Hanoi,
hunchbacked with burdens
of frail sibling humanity,
and my heart was rent by the cluster bombs
and frags that brought this about.

I hid my tri-colored pride
behind an ideogram of this promised land
in another language.   (I had mistakenly held
the notion that war required two parties ...
and now I see only one was there, and for all the
wrong reasons, and am chastened
for my error.)

But sad and feverish, admirable lady, you leave me
astonnished.   I had naïvely thought one
so gifted with words simply
by association through the many galleys, would
acknowledge that adequacy is gained
only when both sides of the paper are written upon.

In rendering your unequivocal judgements, why
have you not told us of the lissome sensuality
of the eighteen-year-old village daughter,
excluded now from the Asian beauty pageant —
and incidentally from life — due to
the imprecise manner in which
her coveted young breasts
were hacked from her body
by a V.C. tax collector
in one summer of coercion?   No doubt
one of Uncle Ho's children, the revolutionary
assailant — one who suffered all for his cause.
For Uncle Ho you disremember so selectively.

I have heard no cries for her father
who was probably no better than he ought be
whose bones yet bleach in the palm-flitted sunlight
of Long Binh (Royal Peace) Province,
his skeletal framework held upright, clasping
in bony arms and xylophonic ribs
the pointed bamboo stake
upon which he was impaled for his
daughter's impertinence, for crying out
when she found she could no longer
suckle his grandchild.

I know from you, if I did not know
before, about the Yankee Doodle
anguish in Vinh
when the vapor-trailing sky dragons have gone.

But where have you explained the fall
from grace, the persistent disregard
of parallel excuses for the patriot sapper team
who planted their charges during Tet '68,
in the walls and ceiling of the Catholic orphanage
in Hue, and locked the children inside
to enjoy the fireworks.   Their frail
academically deprived bodies filled a long ditch.

In a bizarre reversal, it saddens me
more than it angers — and God knows, I have
anger enough — to see again
how self-aggrandizement is all in self-delusion,
and canonizations in the first person
are excluded from all save the shallowest
morality plays where the players
long for other roles.

This one-way rebuttal serves no purpose
beyond purging the residual
sympathy and tolerance
I mistakenly allow to wash upon my heart
between such fairy tales as yours that come
with the seasons.   I have seen them come and go
and the cycles continue.   For every horror
for which I feel guilt, I name you ten
for which I feel anger and hate and despair.

You are too willing to lean upon
my fragile shame ... there was shame enough,
wrong enough, to go around,
and the perpetrators abound

in disregard.   My despair is self-generated, within
by trendy words and I cry'out, not at the futility,
rather at the lie.

But this won't suit your needs, and so
you'll go on to other causes, other
chic and facile icons,
voicing only with voices,
an anti-happening looking for happening with a
casual disregard for the world,
and your ship will tumble off the flat
of the Earth to the applause of only the cast.

With or without concurrence
it comes back to linebreaks
and music, lyricism and secondary images
where the best and worst of your examples
can be found today in greening lands still
ravaged by their own kind —
          and who do you blame now,
now that we're out of the game?

I await your fourth act in this drama,
wherein the leading men have changed
their masques.

## Ward Four: RESTRICTED

War is a communicable disease
which isolation merely exacerbates,
brings back in full fury
all its terminal consequences
to those who contract it,
those who treat it.

Purple heart bearers
and honorees of Arlington's long, slow ride
exhibit more graphic states.
They lie down with honor, a pathetic peace
which sacrifice almost justifies.

In Ward Four the breathing is labored
but quiet.   Beds filled
with Oriental-colored whites, blacks tinged
with green.

*Malaria!* they whisper, passing.

Pus-shaded bottles, swollen membranes
ready for changing.   No head wounds
here, no greenstick fractures, piercing.
Sucking chest wounds go into surgery
or Ward Seven
or the aluminum box.

Ward Four evinces the false promise of
Primaquine.   Between
draining sweats and fevered hallucinations
every member of this white-clad brigade
volunteers to accept the GIs
along with the preventative.

Too late!
An unfavored option no longer available.
Statistical six-out-of-tens
take a route that is one way from this
anesthesiastic gambling salon.

They never made the messhall Tuesdays for lunch.

## Semi-Private Mirages

Mists rise on tidelands,
marsh oats bound the flats in morning
birds poised for seafaring . . .

A desert of red,
taffy-streaked arroyos;
blue stone-breast-pierced skies and
mountains falling away in forests;
the flutter of tabs in downhill *schüss*-ing whispers,
cries like scavengers.

Grass baskets, vegetables, bananas,
prickly pears, and
fish in long narrow boats, clustered
windbells hung in the awkward silence
where the path winds upward beneath
boughs dripping crystals onto spruce carpets,
climbing among mossed palaces.

Mist burns away;
smoke and dust settle;
pliant bamboo stands:
tremulous,
thunder moves off across the river.

A blackened field emerges,
taste of ashes,
grey tissue splashed
pink on the coarse weave of sandbags.

The things
I can remember
come only in flashes.

## Lapsed Lease

Full-fledged commissars
now call home
the haphazard regimentation
of Tan Son Nhut,
Davis Station, The Ritz.

All the friends who died
in Cholon Navy
and Army 3rd Field Hospitals . . .
these portals used now
by the clamoring victors
to treat the VD left behind —
our one getting-even act.

I would be satisfied
with this state of affairs
if only I could know
they cannot make
the phone system work
either.

## 50 Irving Street, N.W.

Must that man be so loud?   Why
is he so demanding — *What is he demanding?*
*I don't think he knows, crowding before*
*me in his anger.*

Hey, America!   I don't want your sympathy.   I want
this form completed,
this contract honored.   It says, right here
on this red-white-and-blue card . . . and now
while all these dregs
lining up for the powdered caressing
of needle marks
and fiery visions that march through their bulletin
bored minds, now . . . I wait.   If I embarrass you
with my unmilitary posture —

*Yes, I hear him.   I have heard his history: two*
*hitches in the Navy, the medical, the shift from*
*God of Abraham to God of Mohammed, recanted, no*
*job he can hold, no family he can keep, inability*
*to sleep, to rationalize — his is as sick,*
*his pain is as great*
*as mine, I know.   But he's loud.*

My posture.   That odd pose, I hear someone say —
*it is my own familiar voice* — is enhanced by the
unwelcome addition of
metric measures of steel from the Urals,
a foreign entity in my case:
I have never been near those Slavic peaks.

The marvelous steel that will not rust sometimes
works its way
enticingly close to the serrated canal
of my spine and creates
this oddly sculptured scarecrow;
pain is merely the medium.

*Schizo!   That is his problem.   I just heard him admit
to classic schizophrenia, as if it was a thing I did
not recognize.   Classic, indeed . . .*

In the cafeteria they circle the room with trays, like
ravenous bombers
homing from hard Kassel runs, seeking
a field alone to land in isolation of their pain and
anguish, and in my confusion, anxious
not to identify with them, I too sit alone.

I cannot be held responsible for one
who may crash on landing, face down
into his scalloped potatoes.   If he wants
alone, he gets alone.   Too far
removed from battlefields, their eyes have a
haunted
self-accusation, nothing to do with guilt.

They slipper by in the halls, GSA-ed into a softshoe
without music.   Play melancholy, baby Clancy.
One more time.

I see now, I know your dispassionate treatment
is the more humane.   How could I
not have recognized that: the mountain of forms
forms a wall, an isolation
device, a stopper of tears,
done for their benefit.   And you
perform in this manner only reluctantly.


     *. . . what clinic?*
*Neural . . . neuralo . . . neu —*
     *Neurosurgery?*
*Yeah, that do sound like it.*
     *Right there.   Room two-oh-six.   Do you have*
     *your routing slip?*
*What kinda' slip?*


Their last hedge against dispossession,
the brown paper bag, brought to Admissions
clutched in communal hands.
The blue property room is wall-to-wall brown
paper bags, residuals
unclaimed from the antiseptic conflicts
under the lights upstairs.


The government issue buffer, a machine of stability
from the garden to Armageddon,
from Gethsemene to Bimini, whirs
in and out among the slippered feet, a lulling
monotone overriding siren loneliness,
cries of pain, cries of . . .
the efficient brushes turn all marks of passage
to swirls in the paste wax residue

along the checkered hallway
where the schizophrenic postulant
demands to leave
because *those people* in Admissions have
a hostile attitude.

Pain is incidental, most abundantly
someone else's: spasmodic clutching
of fevered muscles, twisted tissue.   Burns
are beyond my vision.   The wait is only boring,
not intimidating as they might wish.
Officiousness is aggravating only; after all,
there's no incoming.

But I cannot stand the eyes.   The vacuous
dull staring eyes.   The sightless mummies
pretend they don't know, don't understand.
But they know!   They have felt, somewhere
beneath the empty, drooling stupidity, the slack
mouth and dripping eye, they still feel, even
if only pain.   And the crying out in silent eyes,
realizing no reprieve from their terminal confusion,
eats only on those of us who wish
we had not come.

     *You're not in the pain clinic, are you?*
*I wants to see Doctor Shchuemahn, 'cause he tol'*
*me —*
     *Well, sit.   Just sit.   I'll give it to you . . . just*
*don't persecute me.*

A good cross-section of Americana,
my chair mate offers, putting himself above
the tearing in my guts with words I might have
used.

If I thought as he, I answered,
I would slit my wrists — on some principle.

Rockwell prints on a neutral wallpaper weave.
Across the room, with seats backing
on prints of Boudin's *Return of the Terreneuvier.*
A Fragonard, a Carravaggio, a Jan Davidsz
de Heem.
You must choose your seat with an artistic eye: you
will wait forever in any case.
A Cezanne copy on plastic; Too Loose Lautrec with
high kicking girls of the Rue Pastis.
Stainless steel trash deposits, GSA standard carpet
in barf blue patterns without design, a white
enamel water cooler, waterless,
with ancient rust commenting upon the lip.

Canned Muzak — supermarket music, Denny calls
it: makes you want to run out and buy a can of
peas — and a Conelrad alert
heeded by no one
       (except the seeing-eye dog of the pimp from
       14th Street, who is not blind, but it's a good
       gig to work on the cops and for sympathy).

Someday
when things all work out right
on Irving Street, it will be for real,
and all the zombies will be left for rubble.
Nowhere
to run to
from this last resort.

---

[Note: 50 Irving Street in northwest Washington, DC, is the street address of the capital's Veterans Administration Hospital.]